Contents

Page

LIST OF ILLUSTRATIONS.. iii

LIST OF TABLES.. iv

ACKNOWLEDGMENTS.. v

ABSTRACT vi

INTRODUCTION 1

THE EMERGENCE OF A NEW INTERNATIONAL GIANT 4
    Background to Reform in the PRC 4
    Reaction of the West 6
    The Effect of Economic Reforms on China 7

CHINESE DEFENSE PRODUCTION PRIORITIES 12
    National Defense Priorities and Operational Objectives................... 12
    Recent Changes in China's Military Doctrine and Strategy 13
        Doctrine of "Active Peripheral Defense... 13
        Impact of the Gulf War... 14
    Acquisition Priorities 15

RESOURCES FOR DEFENSE INDUSTRIES 18
    Chinese Defense Spending... 18
        Official Figures 18
    Other Income Sources 20
        PLA Operated Enterprises 20
        Profits from Arms Sales 21
    Defense Industrial Base... 23
        Manufacturing Base 23
        Skilled Personnel Base 24
        Access to High-Technology Resources... 24

MILITARY EQUIPMENT MODERNIZATION 26
    Equipment Modernization.. 27
        Naval and Air Force Modernization.. 27

Impediments to Defense Modernization Efforts..29
    Political and Societal Obstacles 29
    Decrease in Procurement...31
    Government-Run Industries..32
    Management of Defense Industries...33

IMPACT OF MODERNIZATION ON MILITARY CAPABILITY............................35
    Conclusions on Military Modernization 35
    Impact on Military Capability 36

IMPLICATIONS FOR THE UNITED STATES AND THE REGION.........................39

BIBLIOGRAPHY 44

Illustrations

Page

Figure 1. World's Largest Economies (1996) 5

Figure 2. Official Defense Budget of the PRC 19

iii

Tables

Page

Table 1. PLA-Operated Defense Enterprises.. 21

Table 2. Chinese Arms Transfer Agreements with the World 22

Acknowledgments

I express my sincere thanks to Colonel James M. Norris for his help and guidance in completing this research report and to my wife Sandy for assistance in editing it. In addition, the Air University library staff, especially Linda Colding, helped guide me to resources I could never have possibly found on my own. This made this project much easier than I imagined. I truly appreciate all the special assistance I received. Again, thank you.

Abstract

China is experiencing extremely rapid changes in every element of its national power—economic, political, and military. Its economy is booming, producing double-digit gains each year since the mid-1980s. This explosive growth raises the prospect of China emerging as a major global power. To help protect this potential new status, Beijing decided to modernize its military to "gain respect" in the world community and become militarily competitive with other global powers. This resulted in a nation possessing one of the fastest growing economies in the world combined with one of the largest military machines—that is slowly gaining an offensive force-projection capability. These factors may upset the balance of power in the Asian region, in addition to posing a threat to U.S. interests.

This paper examines the implications for U.S. and regional security posed by the economic reforms and the military modernization taking place in China, focusing on Chinese acquisition and indigenous production of high-technology weapons to produce an offensive force projection capability. After surveying the lack of resources available to the Chinese defense industries, it analyzes China's military equipment modernization program and impediments to that program. By assessing the impact of the impediments, it concludes that the economic reform in the People's Republic of China (PRC) has actually slowed military modernization efforts and hindered indigenous defense production. This has reduced the military's possibilities of developing limited or sustained force projection for 15 to 25 years. Thus the U.S. and regional nations have an opportunity to engage China and bring it fully into the world community before it becomes a regional threat.

Chapter 1

Introduction

To get rich is glorious.[1]

—Deng Xiaoping

China began modernizing its military in the early 1980s, intending to update its obsolete post-Korean War equipment with newer, but still "low-tech" weapons. Its objective was to build a force strong enough to counter the threat of a massive land attack from either the United States or the Soviet Union, so it began acquiring this type of weaponry in great numbers.[2] But in the mid-1980s, China also began to reform its economy by gradually adopting a free market system and slowly began opening its doors to the international community. This happened simultaneously with an Asian economic boom that produced double-digit gains in the economy each year for over 10 years, fueling extremely rapid changes in every facet of Chinese national power—economic, political, and military. This explosive growth raised the prospect that China may emerge as a global economic power.[3] To help protect this potential new status, China decided to modernize and expand its indigenous military production capabilities. Until the Chinese could get their industries up to modern standards, the government began purchasing "high-tech" weapons from foreign sources to modernize its navy, air force, and missile infrastructure.[4]

1

As part of the overall modernization program, the Chinese military began shifting their military strategy from homeland defense to force projection. This change was viewed with concern among both the regional powers and the United States. Many people in the United States, including members of Congress, other government and business leaders, scholars, and military officers became concerned about the potential regional security problems posed by the military modernization in China. They fear that Chinese military modernization and economic reform is increasing the People's Liberation Army's (PLA) ability to project offensive forces into neighboring countries. They also fear that the Chinese navy will be able to project force into the South China Sea to establish a regional hegemony. They conclude that an aggressive China will destroy the "economic miracle" that is occurring in Asia, especially among the "Asian Tigers."[5]

However, other regional experts have argued that China is flexing its economic muscle to establish a better life for its citizens and will not exercise its military power. They assert that China's military modernization programs are merely for self-defense, that the PRC is not a threat to the region, and that they will avoid conflict unless directly attacked.[6] Which view is correct? The answer lies someplace between these two views. This paper will attempt to find the answer to this question—specifically, what are the implications for U.S. and regional security posed by the economic reforms and military modernization taking place in the People's Republic of China (PRC)?

This paper will show that the economic reform in the PRC has actually slowed military modernization efforts and hindered indigenous defense production. This has reduced the military's possibilities of developing either limited or sustained offensive force projection for 15 to 25 years. The first chapter looks closely at China, the emerging international economic giant. Then the following chapter examines Chinese defense priorities by showing the changes in national objectives, military strategy and doctrine, and Beijing's new acquisition priorities. After surveying the resources available to the Chinese defense industries, the report analyzes their military equipment modernization program and impediments to that program. The next chapter assesses the state of the defense modernization program. Finally, the last chapter looks at the implications of the modernization program for regional stability, regional security concerns, and U.S. policy.

Notes

[1] Mel Gurtov, "Swords into Market Shares: China's Conversion of Military Industry to Civilian Production," *China Quarterly*, June 1993, 214.

[2] US Defense Intelligence Agency, *Defense Industries in Transition,* PC-1920-59D-95 (Washington, D.C.: Government Printing Office, 1995), 3 – 5.

[3] Hans A. Binnendijk and Patrick L. Clawson, ed., *Strategic Assessment 1997: Flashpoints and Force Structure* (Washington, D.C.: National Defense University, Institute for National Strategic Studies, 1997), 45 – 46.

[4] Zalmay Khalilzad, ed., *Strategic Appraisal 1996* (Santa Monica, Ca.: Rand, 1996), 205-209.

[5] Robert Sutter and Peter Mitchener, *China's Rising Military Power and Influence: Issues and Options for the U.S.* (Washington, D.C.: Congressional Research Service, 1996), 15 – 21.

[6] US Congress, *Global Economic and Technological Change: Former Soviet Union, Central and Eastern Europe and China: Hearings before the Joint Economic Committee,* 103rd Cong., 2d sess., 1994, 34.

Chapter 2

The Emergence of a New International Giant

China's size, increasing wealth, and growing military power ensure that Beijing will play a major role, for good or ill, in every major global issue…[1]

—Senator John McCain

Background to Reform in the PRC

China is experiencing rapid and revolutionary changes in every element of its national power: economic, political, and military.[2] Of these instruments of power, China's leaders place top priority on economic growth. They link their future status as a world power to continued growth.[3] China's growth rates have averaged nearly 10 percent per year since the 1980s. This economic boom resulted in increased living standards for much of the population, an "opening" of the country to the West, increased relations with regional countries, increased expectations of greater wealth, and a strong desire to modernize their society. If the economy continues to grow, China's leaders hypothesize, their influence will soon extend throughout the world.[4]

The transformation of China in the last decade has been truly remarkable. In the early 1980s, China's economic muscle on the world stage was insignificant. Its share of world trade was less than one percent.[5] But today China has an economy with a larger gross domestic product (GDP) than any of the region's countries. Some experts predict that early

4

in the 21st century, the combined GDP of greater China will surpass those of the European Community and the United States.[6] This market-led growth is exerting strong influence on Beijing's diplomatic and security policies. As a result of the growth, China is becoming tied to the international community with expanding links and greater international dependencies.

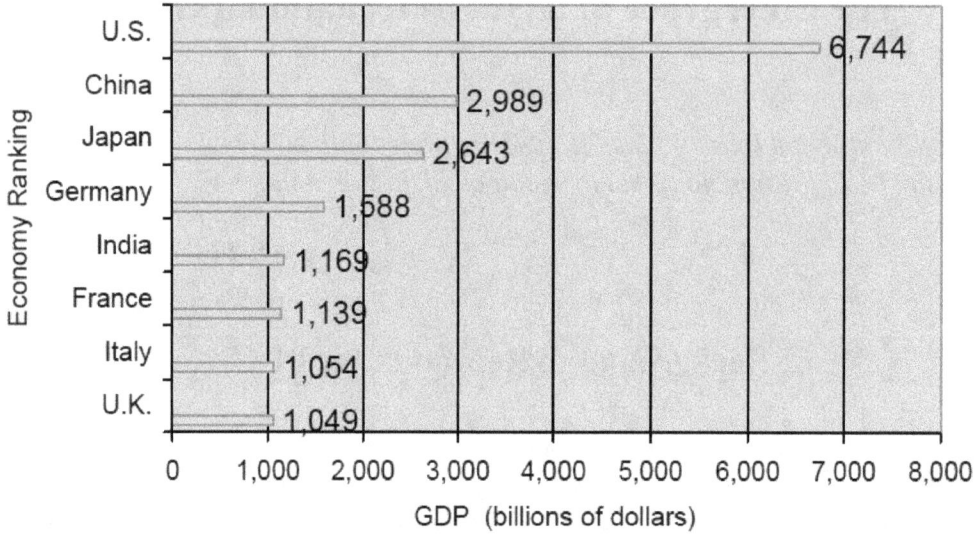

Source: National Defense University, *1997 Strategic Assessment.*

Figure 1. World's Largest Economies (1996)

The former, planned economic system of the Maoist period, with its collectivized agriculture and industrial production through state-run entities, is being replaced by a decentralized, open, and market-driven economy. The transformation brought about revolutionary changes in Chinese levels of production, personal income levels, and government revenues. In addition, millions of Chinese have "tasted" wealth and are increasingly intent on ensuring continued market reforms. China's leaders concur, but their intentions also include modernizing the military. They conclude that if China is to be a true world power, it must have a strong economy *and* a modern military. According to Chinese Defense Minister Chi Haotian, "We must have whatever other big powers have already had in their inventory."[7] His point is that sufficient military power buys both deterrence and status. Therefore, China's intentions are to take some of the "wealth" generated by the market reforms and use it to fuel the military modernization programs.

According to Harry Harding, China is rapidly becoming one of the great powers in Asia, deriving its strength on its *own* military and economic power.[8] Therefore, the world is watching the emergence of a new international giant, making many countries view China's growth with concern.

Reaction of the West

There is a growing wariness in the West regarding the growth and reforms taking place in the PRC. One of the most commonly held beliefs is that the economic reform, combined with the rapid economic growth, makes a positive, direct contribution to the development of China's defense production capabilities.[9] Also, according to this view, the growth contributes to the modernization of the People's Liberation Army (PLA), increasing their capabilities. The West is concerned with military strategy changes, especially the PLA expanding its offensive capabilities. For example, the Chinese are increasing their imports of modern weapons systems and technology. Also, even after personnel reductions of over one million, the PLA's forces still retain over two million people—an enormous force in the region.[10] Chinese economic growth has produced an apparent growth in military spending exceeding Western estimates of Chinese defense expenditures.[11] All this, combined with China's opaqueness in all defense matters, has led to great concern in the West, including the appearance of alarmist literature warning about the regional consequences and threats to U.S. interests as a result of a modern Chinese military.[12]

In addition to the reforms and modernization programs, China has embarked on other programs and operations that increase the concern of the West and of regional nations. They have sold technologies related to weapons of mass destruction (WMD), as well as missile delivery system technology, in sensitive regional hot spots.[13] They supported the nuclear programs of Iran and Pakistan.[14] They built a military installation on a reef in the South China Sea less than 150 miles from the main Philippine Islands, laying claim to islands in the area. China also engages in nuclear testing that other countries have banned, and it has been slow in signing the Comprehensive Test Ban Treaty.[15] Furthermore, China has been aggressive toward Taiwan, firing missiles in the vicinity of the island nation in 1995, resulting in the response of two United States Navy carrier battle groups. These actions do not contribute to the region's sense of peace and stability.

Therefore, there is increasing alarm in the West that the effect of economic reform is building its military capabilities to a point where China will be in a position to dominate the region both economically and militarily. Many analysts argue that the approach the West should take is one of containment, reminiscent of the U.S. policy toward the Soviet Union in the Cold War, and reviving the Southeast Asia Treaty Organization (SEATO).[16] However, this paper will establish that such measures are not necessary because the economic reforms have not actually produced the modern, capable military that many in the West fear.

The Effect of Economic Reforms on China

China's extraordinary economic performance is largely due to strong fundamentals that provide a solid basis for economic growth, a large natural resource base, and a huge domestic market. The Maoist era, contrary to conventional belief, created a basic scientific and industrial infrastructure that can support further modernization.[17] The Communist ideology, however, prevented the Chinese from developing their full potential. The current leaders tapped that potential by dismantling much of the central planning bureaucracy and by allowing market forces to guide the economy. This combination of a more efficient policy harnessing vast economic resources is one reason the economy became supercharged.[18]

China's leaders recognize that to be a player on the world stage, China's strength must be grounded in the development of the national economy and national technological capability, rather than in military capability alone.[19] This past summer, China's Premier Jiang Zemin reiterated the policy of his predecessor, Deng Xiaoping, that the "number one priority of China is economic development."[20] Therefore, military industrial modernization has taken second place to keeping the economic boom hot. Since mid-1994, Beijing has been unable to continue pursuing both economic and military industrial modernization simultaneously.[21] This, coupled with the public's desire to continue to gain wealth, made Beijing begin diverting resources away from the military and defense industries toward civilian pursuits.[22] The PLA leadership also echoed this shift in policy. They accepted the principle that military modernization, including the acquisition of modern weaponry, must await the construction of a strong economy. Therefore, they support the drive for continued economic development. In fact, Liu Huaqing, Vice Chairman of the Central Military Commission and one of the most senior military officers on active duty, recently stated that "building a strong economy is the best path towards building a modern military."[23]

Beijing also states that this development requires a peaceful international environment.[24] In fact, both the civilian leaders in Beijing and military leaders in the PLA want to avoid any conflict unless China's sovereignty is directly challenged.[25] Therefore, except for their policy toward Taiwan, they do not wish to pursue aggressive policies that will lead to international conflict. So China has begun a policy aimed at developing friendly relations with its neighbors. Specifically, they negotiated border agreements with Russia and Kazakhstan, established relations with South Korea, began trade with Taiwan, and improved relations with Vietnam. The government has aggressively assured foreign businesses and leaders that China is stable domestically and is not pursuing war. They have adopted a policy of opening up the country to the outside world. This act forced them to adopt many global rules and regulations that they ignored when they were isolated.[26]

Due in large part to the opening of the country, China handled its leadership succession rather poorly. The Communist ideology is losing appeal to the public, especially the rising middle class.[27] The party has lost the firm control over all economic matters that it once enjoyed. The rapid economic growth is producing new interests and new power centers. New ideas are coming into the country, and with advances in communication, the public sees that the rest of the region's countries are more advanced than China. This is producing great dissent among workers and middle managers in many areas of the country. According to Harry Harding,

> [Economic] modernization and reform are, inevitably, producing severe grievances, particularly with regard to inflation, inequality, unemployment, and corruption. And yet, there are few institutional mechanisms through which those societal interests and popular complaints can be heard and acted upon.[28]

So China's leaders are faced with a problem that is relatively new to China – labor unrest. As a consequence, they have no mechanism to deal with labor disputes except violent suppression of the workers.[29]

In addition, with the disappearance of the Cold War and the demise of the threat of a military invasion, Yan Xuetong, a leading strategic analyst, says that disgruntled workers

9

and ethnic separatism now plague China, with strong ethnic nationalism arising among the populace.[30] The economic reforms allowed these problems to surface over the last five to seven years. So the political leadership is starting to focus on conflict coming from within the country instead of from another nation. The military, in turn, is beginning to shift its focus to crushing internal opposition in attempts to keep the country and economy stable. So China's attention is turning away from harassing their neighbors to one of internal consolidation of power.[31]

The effects of economic reforms resulted in an economic boom for China that showed double-digit economic growth for over 10 years. The reforms allowed China to emerge as a major regional economy and an increasingly larger actor in the global market. It gave rise to increased living standards for much of the population and resulted in opening the country. In the next chapter, we examine how these reforms also created a shift in national priorities. The growth of the economy, the reduction of external threats, the growing influence of public opinion, and the growing internal threats to the political system combined to force China's leaders to make the changes. In addition, we will look at the impact of this shift in priorities on Chinese defense production.

Notes

[1] Kim R. Holmes and James J. Przystup, ed., *Between Diplomacy and Deterrence. Strategies for U.S. Relations with China* ISBN 0-89195-242-X, May 1997, n.p.; on-line, Internet, February 3, 1998, available from http://www.heritage/pubs_library/chinabook/
[2] Zalmay Khalilzad, ed., *Strategic Appraisal 1996* (Santa Monica, Ca.: Rand, 1996), 185.
[3] Hans A. Binnendijk and Patrick L. Clawson, ed., *Strategic Assessment 1997: Flashpoints and Force Structure* (Washington, D.C.: National Defense University, Institute for National Strategic Studies, 1997), 46.
[4] Ibid.
[5] Ling Wu, "Economic Policies," *China Daily,* September 13, 1997.
[6] David Shambaugh, ed., *Greater China: The Next Superpower?* (New York: Oxford University Press, 1995), 1.

Notes

[7] Samuel S. Kim, *China's Quest for Security in the Post-Cold War World* (Carlisle Barracks, Pa: U.S. Army War College, Strategic Studies Institute, 1996), 9.

[8] Harry Harding, "A Chinese Colossus?" *Journal of Strategic Studies* (September 1995), 105.

[9] Bates Gill, "The Impact of Economic Reform Upon Chinese Defense Production," in *Military Modernization*, ed. C. Dennison Lane, et al. (London: T.J. Press, 1996), 144.

[10] Ron Montaperto, "China as a Military Power," *Strategic Forum*, no. 56, December 1995, 2.

[11] James Lilley, "Foreword," in *Military Modernization*, ed. C. Dennison Lane, et al. (London: T.J. Press, 1996), 5.

[12] Harding, 105.

[13] US Senate, *The Growth and Role of the Chinese Military: Hearing before the Subcommittee on East Asian and Pacific Affairs of the Committee on Foreign Relations*, 104th Cong., 1st sess., 1996, 10.

[14] Ibid.

[15] Ibid.

[16] Ibid.

[17] Harding, 106.

[18] Ibid.

[19] John Frankenstein and Bates Gill, "Current and Future Challenges Facing Chinese Defense Industries," *China Quarterly*, June 1996, 389.

[20] Xia Chan, "Jiang Zemin Addresses Party," *China Daily,* June 17, 1997.

[21] US Senate, 46.

[22] Frankenstein and Gill, 389.

[23] US Senate, 47-48.

[24] US Senate, 6.

[25] Montaperto, 1.

[26] US Senate, 7.

[27] Harding, 107.

[28] Harding, 108.

[29] Victor Fung, "The Implications of China's Emergence," in *Overcoming Indifference,* ed. Joseph Cierra (New York: New York University Press, 1995), 259-260.

[30] Kim, 10.

[31] US House, *Security Challenges Posed by China: Hearing before the Committee on National Security*, 104th Cong., 2d sess., 1996, 10.

Chapter 3

Chinese Defense Production Priorities

China does not prepare to establish any force projection capability overseas, does not join in any military alliance, and does not seek spheres of influence; these are important distinguishing qualities of China's armed forces development and defense policy.[1]

—Senior Colonel Wang Zhongchun

There is some truth to the preceding statement. China does not wish to project forces *overseas*, nor does it want to join in alliances. However, Chinese leaders want a force projection capability *in the region* to "defend" the mainland by fighting on the periphery of the country, ideally outside their borders. They also want to exert influence in the South China Sea. In this chapter, we examine this shift in operational strategy and how it resulted in a large list of new priorities for Chinese defense production industries.

National Defense Priorities and Operational Objectives

About 1980, China began a program to break down the barriers between civilian and military production. The program showed initial success for a few years. But the economic boom resulted in the leaders' shifting national priorities from military modernization to keeping the economy hot. This resulted in shifting *away* from military production in favor of the more profitable civilian sector. So the program has undermined defense production as military industries turn their attention toward civilian production.[2]

As noted in the last chapter, the Chinese leadership is committed to building a world-class economy. According to Jiang Zemin, China's premier, the nation's number one priority is economic development.[3] However, they also remain committed to building and fielding a modern military. In fact, both the civilian leaders in Beijing and the leaders of the PLA support the main national objective of assuming the status of a world power.[4] They feel the key to becoming a great power is to build both a strong economy and a modern military. Therefore, to become a world power, China asserts the following national priorities:[5]

1. Economic Development—Free-Market Reforms.
1. Procure, Develop, Build, and Field Modern Military Weapons Systems.
2. Develop Doctrinal Concepts for "High-Tech" Warfare.
3. Maintain Territorial Integrity.
4. Maintain a Stable External Environment—Avoid Conflict.
5. Consolidate Power and Ensure National Unification within China.

China's leaders claim that by accomplishing these national priorities, China will attain "global power" status.[6] In addition, they state that China must be able to compete militarily with all other major powers. The only way they can do this is to modernize military equipment and procedures. They assert that China must strive for stability in the region through negotiation, diplomacy, trade, and cultural exchange. The last task is to ensure stability within China, so the leaders are asking the military for help in quelling any worker, ethnic, or separatist conflict.[7]

Recent Changes in China's Military Doctrine and Strategy

Doctrine of "Active Peripheral Defense

Since the middle 1980s, the PLA has shifted its doctrine away from Mao Tse-Tung's tradition of a land-based, protracted "people's war" defense, which depended greatly on a large army, vast territory, and large population.[8] This doctrine assumed the necessity to defend the country against a land invasion by another state. They would trade space for time and engage in guerilla warfare, followed by a long war of attrition. The PLA's large, antiquated land-based force is inadequate for Chinese defense needs, as external threats have waned. However, their persistent ill feelings toward Japan and the continual United States presence in the area have convinced the Chinese to adopt a strategy of defending the country by projecting forces into the South China Sea.[9] Asserting their sovereignty over areas claimed by Beijing demands improvements in the PLA's capability, including air and naval force projection. Therefore, the PLA has shifted its doctrine to embrace a concept called "active defense," which calls for rapid reaction to limited conflicts along the periphery of the country, attempting to defend the country outside its borders.[10] For example, General Zhang Xusan called for changing the makeup of the PLA force structure to develop the capability to "respond to regional conflict and defending air and sea in distant areas."[11] Therefore, China is acquiring capabilities for force projection, specifically for long range patrolling by air and sea and enforcing Chinese claims to islands in the South China Sea.[12]

Impact of the Gulf War

The emergence of the technology-based battlefield, as China's leaders witnessed in the Gulf War, made another impact on the operational doctrine of the military. In the war, military leaders saw the Coalition forces pummel the Iraqi military. Since much of the Iraqi equipment was Chinese-made, the leaders saw that a revolution in military affairs (RMA) had truly occurred. Sophisticated weaponry such as precision-guided bombs; stealth technology; airborne command and control systems; space-based intelligence; early warning systems; coordinated naval, air, and surface attacks; and real-time command, control and communications capabilities[13] made the PLA's leaders develop a doctrine of "limited war under high-tech conditions."[14] The Gulf War reinforced the PLA's acceptance of the notion that Mao's doctrine of "people's war" was indeed dead.

Therefore, the PLA shifted its military strategy to one of force projection to defend the country outside China's borders and incorporating advanced weaponry to fight this so-called "limited war under high-tech conditions." According to the Ron Montaperto, the Chinese strategists surmised "a future war would be localized, fought to achieve limited political objectives, and won by whichever side is better able to concentrate high-technology force at some distance from the national borders."[15] To accomplish this strategy, China must incorporate a complete change in the way its military is structured. Therefore, this quest for modern weaponry has become vastly important for the military. In fact, equipment modernization has become the PLA's most important priority.[16]

Acquisition Priorities

These changes to Chinese military strategy shift priorities to acquiring a force projection capability—specifically by acquiring advanced air defense systems, anti-ship defenses, and advanced aircraft and naval weapons systems.[17] The PLA has identified key mission areas and weapons systems they must acquire to develop this capability:[18]

1. Developing antisubmarine warfare.
2. Acquiring ship-borne air defense.
3. Building naval capabilities (ships, submarines).
4. Developing equipment for amphibious operations.
5. Developing and fielding modern attack aircraft.
6. Developing and building strategic airlift and air refueling capability.
7. Building modern precision-guided munitions.
8. Developing and fielding modern stand-off weapons such as cruise missiles.
9. Developing and fielding modern command, control, and communications capabilities.[19]

Chinese leaders have placed these force projection modernization efforts at the top of the military's priorities. The PLA leaders recognize that they need robust command, control, and communications systems, coupled with precision munitions, if they are to compete with modern military forces. China's intention is to build these systems indigenously. So Beijing is beginning to allocate additional money to the state-run defense industries in an attempt to convert them into modern weapons producing industries.[20]

China incorporated these new indigenous defense production priorities into their overall military modernization program in 1992.[21] According to Bates Gill, China's "effort [toward self reliance] has been particularly acute."[22] However, he also observes that

> China has traditionally lagged behind other major weapons producers in terms of technological development, in part a function of the country's reluctance to become overly dependent on foreign suppliers. Today as production "goes global" and technology spirals upward in cost and sophistication, Chinese defense industries can ill afford such a parochial understanding of international relations.[23]

Therefore, to enable China to project forces as required by the new national defense priorities, it must first modernize its defense industries and manufacturing processes. To become self-reliant in the manufacture of modern weaponry, it must first seek help from other weapons producing nations. However, until the mid-90s, Beijing has been hesitant to fully seek this "outside" assistance. In the next chapter, we will examine how this policy affected Chinese defense industries. In addition, we will look at the resources available to the defense industries for their modernization efforts, including funds, materials, and personnel.

Notes

[1] David Shambaugh and Wang Zhongchun, *China's Transition into the 21st Century: U.S. and PRC Perspectives* (Carlisle Barracks, Pa.: U.S. Army War College, Strategic Studies Institute, 1996), 37.

Notes

[2] James Lilley, "Foreword," in *Military Modernization*, ed. C. Dennison Lane, et al. (London: T.J. Press, 1996), 9.

[3] Chihai Lichu, "New Directions from Beijing," *China Daily,* June 17, 1997.

[4] Ron Montaperto, "China as a Military Power," *Strategic Forum*, no. 56, December 1995, 2.

[5] Sperric Rejeako, "China Changes Course," *China Watch,* March 1993.

[6] Xiano Weileng, "Premier Draws Praise," *China Daily,* January 4, 1993.

[7] Alfredo Aporcho, "Worker Unrest Grows," *China Watch,* June 1996.

[8] Richard A. Bitzinger and Bates Gill, *Gearing Up for High-Tech Warfare? Chinese and Taiwanese Defense Modernization and Implications for Military Confrontation Across the Taiwan Strait, 1995-2005* (Washington, D.C.: Center for Strategic and Budgetary Assessments, 1996), 8.

[9] Ibid.

[10] Monterperto, 3.

[11] Shulong Chu, "The PRC Grids for Limited, High-Tech War," *Orbis*, Spring 1994, 187.

[12] Bitzinger and Gill, 8.

[13] Zalmay Khalilzad, ed., *Strategic Appraisal 1996* (Santa Monica, Ca.: Rand, 1996), 194-195.

[14] John Frankenstein and Bates Gill, "Current and Future Challenges Facing Chinese Defense Industries," *China Quarterly*, June 1996, 399.

[15] Montaperto, 2.

[16] Ibid.

[17] Bitzinger and Gill, 9.

[18] Hans A. Binnendijk and Patrick L. Clawson, ed., *Strategic Assessment 1997: Flashpoints and Force Structure* (Washington, D.C.: National Defense University, Institute for National Strategic Studies, 1997), 50.

[19] Ibid.

[20] Ti Chagchu, "Defense Industries Help Country," *China Daily,* September 16, 1997.

[21] Albert Smith, "Chinese Industries Enter the Free-Market," *The New York Times on the Web,* November 3, 1997, n.p.; on-line, Internet, November 16, 1997, available from http///www.nytimes.com/03-11-97.

[22] Bates Gill, "The Impact of Economic Reform Upon Chinese Defense Production," in *Military Modernization*, ed. C. Dennison Lane, et al. (London: T.J. Press, 1996), 145.

[23] Gill, 145-146.

Chapter 4

Resources for Defense Industries

Combine the military and the civil, combine peace and war, give priority to military products, let the civil support the military.[1]

—Deng Xiaoping

Chinese Defense Spending

Official Figures

China's defense modernization program has included significant increases in military spending since 1990.[2] The allocation for the military in the official national budget has risen from 25.2 billion yuan (US $6 billion) in 1989 to over 70 billion yuan (US $8 billion, adjusted for inflation) in 1996, thereby more than doubling in only seven years, and showing double-digit increases every year. The main reason for the spending increase was for the defense industrial modernization program, instituted to acquire technologically advanced military forces.[3] According to Ron Montaperto, "because the Chinese do not reveal all of their expenditures on defense, the figures must include an estimate of funds available from other sources. Most outside observers accept estimates of US $20-25 billion."[4] Some estimates are as high as $37 billion.[5]

The official defense budget is only a fraction of the total financial resources available to the Chinese military. A separate fund for defense industries,[6] a fund for military

18

pensions, special grants for precision weapons acquisitions, provincial allocations to local military forces, profits from arms sales and PLA enterprises, allocations to the defense industries under the State Council, and the value of food that military units raise for their own use also provide income for the military.[7]

If placed in perspective, however, these budget increases do not represent a large increase in money available to the defense sector. The double-digit increases in defense spending after 1989 followed at least 10 years of defense budget stagnation. The defense allocation in 1979 was about 20 billion yuan and remained in the 20 billion range until 1989. Because of the high inflation that China experienced throughout the 1980s, the total defense allocation in real terms actually declined. Therefore, most of the increases were offset by high inflation, approaching 20 percent, that continued through the early 1990s.[8] In real terms, this means that China's defense allocation has declined to less than 10 percent of China's GDP today, one of the lowest levels in more than a decade.[9]

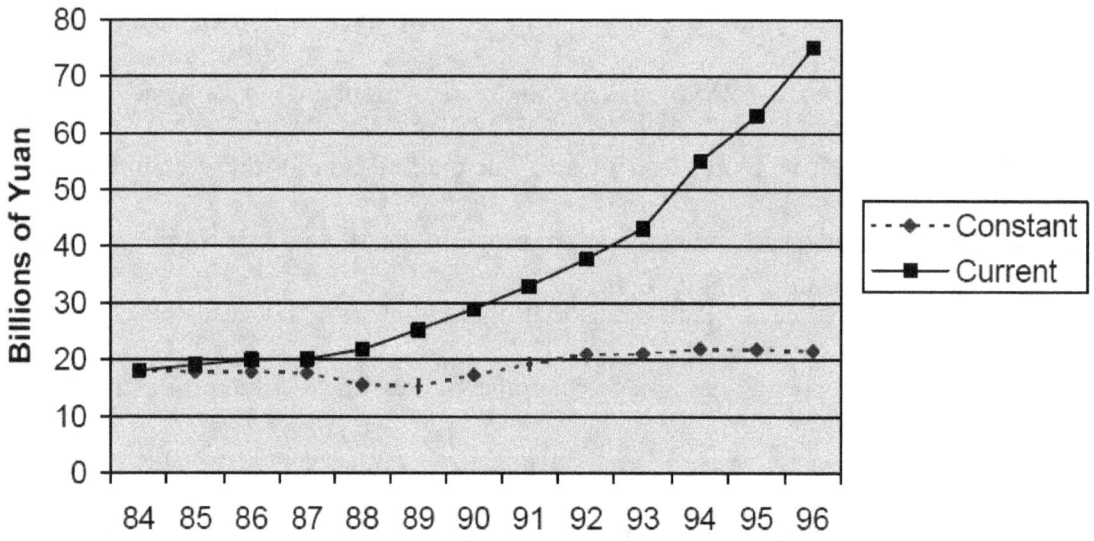

Sources: SIPRI Yearbook 1997 and U.S. Senate Hearings October 11, 1995.

Figure 2. Official Defense Budget of the PRC

Other Income Sources

PLA Operated Enterprises

Not all the military's sources of revenue have increased. Indeed, the "official" budget has increased, but other sources of the PLA's income have declined. To help fuel the modernization program, the PLA began searching for alternative funding sources in the early 1980s to boost its income. One of the programs Beijing tried was defense conversion—a program in which some defense manufacturing plants began to produce civilian products or consumer goods. The result was that a significant portion of the military defense industries began producing civilian products and came under control or ownership of the PLA.[10] Commercial enterprises owned by the PLA include transnational pharmaceutical corporations, automobile and truck production, mining, real estate development, hotels, restaurants, airline and shipping services, and many other activities, including currency futures deals. The PLA is also involved in the construction of economic development zones in major trading centers, capitalizing on the economic boom.[11] From the businesses operated by the PLA, there are significant profits. But how much of these profits actually go to fuel the defense budget is not clear. The Chinese claim that more than 50 percent of the profits go toward reinvestment. Of the remaining amount, they claim that most goes toward general services such as feeding and billeting the troops.

Chinese officials also assert that nearly one-third of all commercial enterprises operated by the PLA operate at a loss. Western experts verify this assertion and suggest that the actual numbers may be much greater. There are widespread reports that many officers have been corrupted by commerce and siphon off profits for personal use. So widespread is the corruption that in 1996, lower level military units were ordered to stop commercial operations completely.[12] According to Ron Montaperto, if these funds were

withheld, the military could lose nearly one-quarter of its budget and the difference would

have to be made up from the shrinking pool of official funds.[13]

Table 1. PLA-Operated Defense Enterprises

DEFENSE INDUSTRY	MILITARY PRODUCTS	CIVILIAN PRODUCTS
Ministry of Nuclear Industry	Nuclear Weapon Material	Nuclear Power Plant Reactors, Optical Instruments, Mining Equipment, Air Filters, Valves, Heat Exchangers
Ministry of Aviation	Fighters, Bombers, Transports, Helicopters, Engines	Agricultural Planes, Prototype Commercial Aircraft, Boeing 757 Cargo Doors, Tourist Buses, Refrigerators, Washing Machines, Clocks, Air Conditioners, Automobiles, Tobacco Machines, Ovens
Ministry of Electronics	Avionics, Radar, Sonar, C3I Equipment, Missile Navigation Systems, Communication Gear	Consumer Electronics, Computers, Copying Machines, Ice Skates, Lamps, Electric Meters, Processing Machines, Washing Machines
Ministry of Ordnance Industry	Tanks, Armored Personnel Carriers, Anti-tank Weapons, Artillery, Mortars, Rocket Launchers, Rifles, Anti-aircraft/ Ship Missiles	Metal Cutting Tools, Precision Machinery, Bicycles, Chemical Products, Electric Appliances, Furniture, Motorcycles, Gas and Pressure Cylinders, Heavy Trucks, Railway Cars
China State Shipbuilding Corporation.	Submarines, Destroyers, Frigates, Fast Attack Craft, Patrol Escorts, Mine-sweepers, Hydrofoils, Landing Craft, Communication Gear	Bulk Carriers, Diesel Engines, Container Vessels, Offshore Drilling Rigs, Engineering and Consulting Services, Fishing Vessels
Ministry of Space Industry	Strategic Weapons Systems, ICBMs, IRBMs, MRBMs, Tactical Missiles, Anti-ship Missiles	Communications, Meteorological Satellites, Remote Sensing Instruments, Cameras, Launch Vehicles, Televisions, Batteries, Medical Products, Ovens, Automobile Parts

Sources: Srikanth Kondapalli, "China's Defense Industry," in *Strategic Analysis*, September 1996, p. 870; Wei-chin Lee, "China's Defense Industry Invades Private Sector," in *SAIS Review*, Summer-Fall 1995, 200.

Profits from Arms Sales

In the late-1980s, China was selling as much as $4.7 billion dollars in weapons to

developing countries. Many analysts predicted that the Chinese arms exports would expand, resulting in huge profits for the defense modernization programs or for purchasing high-tech foreign equipment.[14] However, as shown in Table 2, by 1991 Chinese sales dropped to a mere $110 million, largely as a result of the end of the Iran-Iraq war. Another negative influence on sales was that Chinese equipment became unattractive to the world after the Gulf War. The Iraqis operated many Chinese weapons systems such as tanks, air defense systems, and radar systems. These unsophisticated systems were no match for Coalition forces or Western military equipment. This resulted in a significant drop in orders for Chinese military equipment. Therefore, profits from arms sales currently account for very little in the overall defense budget of China.

Table 2. Chinese Arms Transfer Agreements with the World

(In millions of current US dollars)

1986	1987	1988	1989	1990	1991	1992	1993	1994	1995	1996
1,800	4,700	2,500	1,600	2,300	110	300	400	400	550	250

Sources: Richard F. Grimmett, *Conventional Arms Transfers to the Third World,* (Congressional Research Service, July 29, 1994), p. 83 and *SIPRI Yearbook 1997* (Oxford University Press, 1997), Table 9.1.

In addition to losses to inflation, loss of profits from PLA enterprises, and lower arms sales income, much of the recent increase in military spending has gone into salary hikes for the PLA officer corps—some receiving more than a 50 percent increase.[15] The increases were to compensate for inflation and to prevent officers from leaving the service for more financially rewarding opportunities in the civilian sector. Other personnel programs and quality of life initiatives such as building new barracks have taken up much of the increases as well. Overall, inflation and other programs have significantly eroded the amount of money available to the Chinese military equipment modernization program.

Defense Industrial Base

Manufacturing Base

According to Bitzinger and Gill, China has one of the oldest and largest military-industrial complexes in the world. The system of defense industries comprises more than 2000 enterprises, factories, and research centers. In addition, these industries have achieved a high degree of self-reliance largely due to the closed Communist society of the 1940s –1970s.[16] They state that the Chinese defense industries are one of the world's few producers of a full range of military systems.

China has an adequate infrastructure for the defense industries. The facilities are in relatively good shape, transportation is excellent, and raw materials are relatively abundant. They have more than enough manpower for unskilled labor and craftsmen, but they are experiencing shortages in skills needed for high-technology production. The defense industries are excellent for turning out vast quantities of basic military hardware or weapons systems that are adequate for attrition-based wars. However, the industrial base is deficient in high-technology resources and the defense technology base is small.[17] Also, the Chinese have not been able to absorb high-technology manufacturing equipment within their defense industries to an appreciable degree. Kondapalli cites "poor [high-tech] production and quality-control methods, limited standardization procedures, inadequate machine tools, limited instrumentation, and shortages of special materials and metals" needed for production of modern military equipment.[18] Also, as mentioned in a previous chapter, Beijing was hesitant to seek advanced technology production methods and equipment from other nations until the mid-1990s. Thus, they have been unable to exploit advanced technology in their manufacturing practices.

Skilled Personnel Base

A significant problem facing the defense industry as it attempts to modernize is the so-called "brain-drain." All over China, professionals and engineers are leaving the state-run defense industries for more lucrative opportunities in the private sector. This has resulted in a shortage of engineers and technicians needed to help modernize the industrial base to allow indigenous production of the modern weaponry the Chinese leadership desires. Wendy Frieman observes, "The military sector might still have some of the best, but it no longer has all of the best, of China's scientists."[19]

Access to High-Technology Resources

China also faces the problem of gaining access to the technology that can contribute to improving their indigenous defense production.[20] Since the Chinese are limited by their own financial constraints and by the export controls of foreign sources, Chinese purchases of foreign technology will remain small in the future. They are planning to take these purchases and "reverse-engineer" or integrate them into indigenous processes.[21] Even if they plan to do this, China will be limited in their effectiveness because of sanctions imposed on it from countries that supply advanced-technology equipment. The result is that China cannot expect to easily obtain the modern technologies necessary for the "reverse-engineering" processes.

Overall, resources available for indigenous defense production in China remain limited. The defense budget, while showing significant increases, is weakened by inflation and diversion to quality-of-life programs. Profits from the PLA enterprises have been greatly reduced, including the total abandonment of some enterprises by PLA units. Arms sales to third world countries are significantly lower after the Gulf War. The defense industrial base has plentiful resources for traditional "low-tech" military equipment, but it falls short in equipment, personnel, and processes when attempting to develop high-tech weapons. In the next chapters, we will examine how China has put these resources to work in their military equipment modernization program and how the program has fared.

Notes

[1] Orville Schell, *Discos and Democracy. China in the Throes of Reform* (New York: Pantheon Books, 1988), 127.

[2] Zalmay Khalilzad, ed., *Strategic Appraisal 1996* (Santa Monica, Ca.: Rand, 1996), 204.

[3] Charles Pondelton, ed., *World Statistics, 1997* (New York, N.Y.: Random House, 1997), 245 - 251.

[4] Ron Montaperto, "China as a Military Power," *Strategic Forum*, no. 56, December 1995, 3.

[5] Pondelton, 245.

[6] US Senate, *The Growth and Role of the Chinese Military: Hearing before the Subcommittee on East Asian and Pacific Affairs of the Committee on Foreign Relations,* 104th Cong., 1st sess., 1996, 23.

[7] US House, *Security Challenges Posed by China: Hearing before the Committee on National Security*, 104th Cong., 2d sess., 1996, 22.

[8] Ibid.

[9] Hans A. Binnendijk and Patrick L. Clawson, ed., *Strategic Assessment 1997: Flashpoints and Force Structure* (Washington, D.C.: National Defense University, Institute for National Strategic Studies, 1997), 47.

[10] US Senate, 101.

[11] Ibid.

[12] Ibid.

[13] Montaperto, 3.

[14] US Defense Intelligence Agency, *Defense Industries in Transition,* PC-1920-59D-95 (Washington, D.C.: Government Printing Office, 1995), 11.

[15] Montaperto, 3.

[16] Richard A. Bitzinger and Bates Gill, *Gearing Up for High-Tech Warfare? Chinese and Taiwanese Defense Modernization and Implications for Military Confrontation Across the Taiwan Strait, 1995-2005* (Washington, D.C.: Center for Strategic and Budgetary Assessments, 1996), 16.

[17] Srikanth Kondapalli, "China's Defense Industry," *Strategic Analysis*, September 1996, 877.

[18] Ibid.

[19] Bates Gill, "The Impact of Economic Reform Upon Chinese Defense Production," in *Military Modernization*, ed. C. Dennison Lane, et al. (London: T.J. Press, 1996), 155.

[20] Gill, 158.

[21] Ibid.

Chapter 5

Military Equipment Modernization

We shall not yield to any outside pressure or enter into alliance with any group of countries, nor shall we establish any military bloc, join in the arms race, or seek military expansion.[1]

—Jiang Zemin
Speech—September 12, 1997

As noted in a previous chapter, military equipment modernization has become the PLA's number one priority. The leadership in Beijing also espouses a strong desire to produce the new military equipment indigenously. Also, we saw that they are pouring more money into their defense industries in hopes of producing this modern equipment within the country. But lack of resources and slow conversion of the defense industries has thus far enabled them only to *purchase* high-tech weaponry from *outside* China in hopes of "reverse-engineering" the technology. They have also purchased dual-use technologies in hopes of converting the concepts or devices to military application. In this section, we will look at the equipment modernization effort and see if it has translated into the force projection capability the leaders desire. Also, we will see if they have been able to produce the technologies indigenously. Finally, we will examine the impediments to the defense industries' equipment modernization efforts.

Equipment Modernization

The vast majority of the PLA's conventional weapons are rugged, reliable equipment based on 1940s and 1950s technology. They continue to rely on modernized versions of obsolescent Soviet and Chinese equipment. But even after extensive modernization to existing weapons systems, such as improving the avionics, fire control, and power plant and adding modern missile systems, a MiG-21 remains a post-Korean War aircraft that stands little chance against the F-16s flown by other regional powers.[2] Another major problem the Chinese military faces is the obsolescence of a large amount of other military equipment in the near future. The military has vast numbers of tanks and airplanes that were built in the 1950s and 1960s and are nearing the end of their service. Shultz predicts that nearly 4500 airplanes will have to leave the service in the next 5 to 10 years.[3] This is just one example – old equipment is found throughout the Chinese military. Therefore, in addition to desiring advanced technology equipment to modernize and upgrade their forces, China must acquire new equipment to replace the existing force structure.

Naval and Air Force Modernization

According to the Rand Corporation's *Strategic Appraisal 1996*, "Beijing's arms and technology acquisitions in the 80s and 90s have been keyed to the creation of much smaller but highly proficient naval and air forces and related capabilities required for rapid reaction and limited power projection."[4] Since they have not been able to produce advanced technology equipment indigenously, they have acquired equipment from outside sources to supplement their indigenous production efforts. Over the last several years China has taken the following modernization actions:[5]

27

1. Acquired a new, specialized class of destroyer (Luhu), adding 3 ships to the fleet. These vessels possess significant offensive and defensive missile capabilities.
2. Added a new class of frigate (Jiagwei), acquiring 4 vessels.
3. Purchased 26 SU-27 fighter aircraft from Russia. They have the option to buy 48 more in addition to purchasing the technology that will allow them to produce the aircraft indigenously.
4. Purchased 10 IL-76 transport aircraft from Russia.
5. Reportedly purchased air-refueling capability from Israel or Iran that has not yet become operational.
6. Modernized up to 30 B-6 naval bombers that can now carry C-601 anti-ship missiles and 130 A-5 light bombers that are now equipped with torpedoes.
7. Developed mobile, conventional warhead missiles that have a range of 1000 miles. Some were used in live-fire exercises near Taiwan in 1995.
8. Purchased four sophisticated Kilo class submarines from Russia and may acquire 18 more.
9. Reportedly agreed to buy 22 diesel-powered submarines from various countries in the next few years.
10. Reportedly planning to construct or purchase one or two aircraft carriers for deployment between 2010 and 2020.
11. Continue to build about 40 J-7 and 12 J-8 fighter aircraft a year.
12. Purchased and built equipment to allow some units an amphibious capability.

This modernization effort has increased China's military capability, although not significantly. According to Ron Montaperto, these modernization efforts have given China the ability to deploy and conduct limited amphibious operations beyond China's borders. But the units' small size, their dispersal throughout the country, and lack of lift capability limit the effectiveness for large-scale operations.[6] The navy significantly improved its operational range, firepower, and air-defense capabilities. These improvements allow the navy to operate farther from the coast for longer periods.[7] However, the navy still cannot mount sustained, coordinated operations.[8] The air force still has very limited capability, even with the purchase of the advanced Russian fighters. These aircraft, while modern, do not compare to the F-16s possessed by other regional nations. The Chinese have not yet been able to reverse-engineer the advanced fighter for production within China. In addition, spare parts are a problem, since they must purchase the parts from Russia. It takes many months to get spare parts orders filled for these aircraft. Any major maintenance on these planes must be performed at a depot facility within Russia. Also the Chinese have not been able to develop and field an air refueling capability. Even though they purchased transport aircraft, the number of aircraft is too small to give the military any appreciable airlift capability. Their newest indigenously produced fighter, the J-8, has numerous engine and fuel-consumption problems and poor weapons systems.[9] According to the Rand Corporation's *Strategic Appraisal 1996*, "Beijing's effort to develop an advanced indigenous fighter and combat aircraft industry has been largely unsuccessful, and there are few signs of a breakthrough occurring in at least the near future."[10]

Impediments to Defense Modernization Efforts

China has a huge defense complex, supported by a large research and development infrastructure and growing civilian-sector high technology industries. Yet China still cannot produce and deploy advanced weapons systems.[11] In a previous section, we saw some impediments to modernization efforts due to lack of certain resources for the defense industry. In this section, we will examine other impediments to Chinese defense modernization efforts.

Political and Societal Obstacles

One of the largest impediments to the defense industries' attempt at modernization involves political and societal obstacles. Recall from a previous section that the Chinese leadership in Beijing changed the national priorities. Military modernization efforts became secondary to developing the national economy. This political shift in priorities caused major changes in Chinese society. The economic boom of the 1980s became the rush to profits of the 1990s. Throughout society the emphasis was on maintaining market reforms.

This spilled over into the defense sector, whose managers made cases for converting much of their production to civilian goods and services, forcing defense production into quantitative decline. According to Bates Gill, "One Chinese researcher claims that over 85 percent of the output value of the military electronics industry was in civilian products; 83 percent of the value of military production of the shipbuilding industry was in civilian products; 69 percent of the value of the military aviation industry was civilian production; and 64.5 percent of the value of the military ordnance industry was in civilian products."[12] In fact, the official aim of the Chinese defense industry is to reach an average commercial output value of 80 percent by 1999.[13] With as much as 90 percent of the defense production capacity lying idle, and 80 percent of the remaining capacity earmarked for civilian production, the quantity of military production is exceptionally low.[14] This military-to-civilian conversion had a detrimental effect on military production capabilities. Bitzinger and Gill, in discussing Chinese defense industries, observed,

> China's 15-year old economic reform process has, paradoxically, impeded progress in harnessing advanced technologies for military uses. The economic reform measures…have done much to strengthen China, but… this process has also had a debilitating effect on Chinese defense production. Geographically dispersed, hemorrhaging money, with military-related production down to 10 percent of capacity, and badly in need of management skills, the state-run factories concerned with defense production are largely unable to take advantage of the so-called "defense conversion" process, let alone the broader reforms and transformation of the Chinese economy.[15]

In addition, there has been a rising middle class that has become very vocal in Chinese society. They have tasted "wealth" and want the Chinese leaders to take more state money away from defense pursuits so it can be invested in continued market reform. Also, much of the business community within China is generally euphoric over this new-found wealth and have found markets for their goods and services outside the state-run defense industries. The profits are greater in selling their products to the civilian free-market sector than in selling them to state-run enterprises. This has resulted in a marked decrease in materials and services (such as transportation) upon which the defense industry relies. Therefore, according to Frankenstein, in shifting from socialism to a market economy, the defense industries have been forced to move away from defense production.[16]

Decrease in Procurement

Another effect of the economic modernization on the quantitative decline in defense production is a decrease in procurement. With the shift of priorities to economic reform and the change in military strategy, the amount of defense procurement has fallen off significantly. Bates Gill cites four possible reasons for the downturn. First, the cutback of more than one million troops from the PLA has reduced the amount of material needed for the military. Second, the numbers of combat aircraft orders have fallen considerably. Chinese aircraft lack the technology necessary on the modern battlefield, so the PLAAF has been procuring Russian equipment. Therefore, they decreased their orders for the older generation Chinese aircraft produced by indigenous defense industries. Third, the Chinese are not getting as many arms export orders since the Gulf War, as previously mentioned. Therefore, production for arms exports is significantly lower. Finally, there is indecision within the aircraft industry whether to produce advanced Russian fighters indigenously or co-produce them with the Russians. This has slowed production and resulted in less procurement.[17]

Government-Run Industries

A major impediment to the defense modernization effort results from Beijing's insistence that defense industries remain "state-run." This does not allow them access to the competitive markets. As a result, they are losing large sums of money. In 1996, according to official figures, out of a total loss of 441 billion yuan in state-run enterprises, about one-third belonged to the defense industries.[18] In fact, most of the defense industries do not generate enough capital to survive on their own without direct intervention and funding from the state. But following the end of the Cold War, government investment in defense industries significantly declined. This was not only due to a decrease in the threat of a superpower conflict, but also due to the remote locations of many of the industries. According to Frankenstein, in the 1960s and 1970s many defense industries were relocated to remote mountain areas in the interior of China for Cold War security reasons.[19] Today, Chinese national investment in those industries goes mostly for infrastructure—roads, railroads, communication, and tunnels. These four items absorb more than 80 percent of available funds, leaving only a small amount for operations.[20] For example, of the state-run defense industries, nearly 70 percent of the factories are unable to meet salaries on a regular basis. This caused an exodus of personnel out of the defense sector. Like the engineers mentioned previously, many unskilled and semi-skilled workers are relocating to the economic centers on the "gold coast" or to other money-making enterprises.

Management of Defense Industries

The final impediment to defense modernization is the management of defense industries. According to Gill, "It is apparent that the industries are ill-prepared to meet the challenges and opportunities presented by the economic reform and modernization program. Military research, military industrial production, and military procurement still make insufficient use of market resources."[21] Since the defense industries were a closed system that for many years enjoyed a special status immune from the demands of reform, current attempts to introduce reform and new management techniques have not had much success. The old management style still permeates them, and according to one Chinese expert, a change for the better in the system will require the "efforts by a generation of people."[22]

Therefore, the Chinese defense industries still have a long way to go before their modernization efforts will enable them to develop third-generation weapons systems indigenously. Also, they have been unable to reverse-engineer foreign countries' technology for internal production. So until they advance further, the Chinese must rely solely on equipment purchased from foreign sources to modernize their military. In the next chapter, we will assess how these factors shaped China's defense modernization effort, impacted its military capability, and affected Asian regional stability.

Notes

[1] "Jiang: U.S. Has Nothing to Fear," *Associated Press On-Line*, November 1, 1997, n.p.; on-line, Prodigy News Service, November 6, 1997.

[2] John Shultz, Testimony to US Senate, *The Growth and Role of the Chinese Military: Hearing before the Subcommittee on East Asian and Pacific Affairs of the Committee on Foreign Relations*, 104th Cong., 1st sess., 1996, 100.

[3] Ibid.

[4] Zalmay Khalilzad, ed., *Strategic Appraisal 1996* (Santa Monica, Ca.: Rand, 1996), 205-206.

Notes

[5] Shultz, 84 and Khalilzad, 205-211.

[6] Ron Montaperto, "China as a Military Power," *Strategic Forum*, no. 56, December 1995, 2.

[7] Khalilzad, 206-212.

[8] Montaperto, 4.

[9] Khalilzad, 205-211.

[10] Khalilzad, 208-209.

[11] Richard A. Bitzinger and Bates Gill, *Gearing Up for High-Tech Warfare? Chinese and Taiwanese Defense Modernization and Implications for Military Confrontation Across the Taiwan Strait, 1995-2005* (Washington, D.C.: Center for Strategic and Budgetary Assessments, 1996), 21.

[12] Bates Gill, "The Impact of Economic Reform Upon Chinese Defense Production," in *Military Modernization*, ed. C. Dennison Lane, et al. (London: T.J. Press, 1996), 151.

[13] Ibid.

[14] Ibid.

[15] Bitzinger, 22.

[16] John Frankenstein and Bates Gill, "Current and Future Challenges Facing Chinese Defense Industries," *China Quarterly*, June 1996, 426.

[17] Gill, 152-153.

[18] Srikanth Kondapalli, "China's Defense Industry," *Strategic Analysis*, September 1996, 878.

[19] Frankenstein and Gill, 403.

[20] Ibid.

[21] Gill, 156.

[22] Gill, 156-157.

Chapter 6

Impact of Modernization on Military Capability

The PLA fails to meet the needs of modern warfare and this is the principal problem with army-building.[1]

—Senior Vice-Chairman Liu Huaquing

Conclusions on Military Modernization

China's military modernization effort, in contrast to its economic reforms, has been very slow—slower than most Western estimates of the early 1990s. The economic boom and the resulting shift in national priorities from military modernization to economic reform caused a fundamental change in thinking among both the leaders and much of the population. They now conclude that the key to becoming a regional and world power is not through ideology or military might; it is through a strong, thriving economy. Therefore, they want to avoid any type of conflict—short of a direct threat to their sovereignty.[2] They surmised that conflict would derail their quest for greater economic power, so they diverted vast financial resources away from the defense industries and converted a large percentage of each industry to civilian production. Although they are embarking on a robust military modernization program to build a force that would be on par with other modern nations, they are not preparing for superpower conflict. Instead, China's leaders are concerned with internal security and regional influence—specifically blocking Taiwan's independence and laying claims to territory in the South China Sea.[3] Although smaller than originally planned, they earmarked double-digit increases in defense spending to modernize their defense industries and military. Most of the increase in defense spending has gone to salary hikes to the officer corps, to an increase in quality-of-life programs, and to offset inflation. In addition, they have lost revenue from arms exports following the Gulf War, and the PLA-run enterprises are not producing enough income for modernizing their industries.

Therefore, China's indigenous defense production capabilities have not improved. They are still able to produce 1960-era equipment, but they are unable to produce modern weaponry. In addition, acquiring complete systems from foreign sources is not likely to produce vast increases in military capability.[4] They have not been able to absorb these technologies into their industries and reverse-engineer them, thereby eliminating the possibility of indigenous production in the near future.[5] According to Swanson Smith, "The Chinese defense industries are at least a decade away from manufacturing high-tech weaponry on their own."[6] Also, Beijing cannot buy the quantities of foreign high-tech weaponry they need to have the sustained force-projection capability they desire.[7] The expense of these weapons systems is too great for China to afford. Also, since many spare parts come from other countries such as Russia, these parts are not always available. And whether obtained through domestic production or foreign sources, the absorption of advanced weaponry requires more advanced levels of education than the Chinese military currently possesses.[8]

Impact on Military Capability

Overall, even with the slow pace of military reform, the modernization effort *has* improved military capabilities to a small extent. Ron Montaperto states that the PLA is slowly improving but "doctrinal and financial deficiencies will delay the PLA's ability to conduct *sustained* force projection for at least a decade."[9] This power projection will be limited to the South China Sea and the Asian landmass. The modernization of naval forces has enabled China to venture beyond their coastal areas, and may have given them the ability to blockade Taiwan.[10] Therefore, China has accomplished at least one short-term objective – to influence the decisions of Taiwan's leaders.[11] In addition, equipment modernization of air forces has given the PLAAF the capability to intercept aircraft over Mainland China. However, even with the naval and air modernization, the PLA still cannot effectively project forces beyond its borders and is inadequate to defend the country against ground attack. According to the Rand Corporation's *Strategic Appraisal 1996*, "China will likely require a significantly long time (i.e., *at least* 15 to 25 years) to attain a truly modern force structure and operational capability capable of challenging the U.S. military presence in the region."[12]

The appraisal also states that China must overcome many serious technical and organizational problems plaguing its equipment modernization program before they can attain the kind of military capabilities they desire.[13] However, it also cautions that even modest improvements in China's power projection capabilities could generate serious instabilities in the region. For example, a breakthrough in just one high-tech system, such as developing accurate cruise missiles, could give China a significant advantage in the region. Bitzinger and Gill concur, adding that China possesses vast numbers of men and equipment. While the equipment is old, there is a "certain quality to be found in quantity."[14] This means that China is still a formidable force, and if regional countries engage them militarily, and China is able to absorb large losses in men and equipment, then their limitations in high-tech weaponry would be relatively meaningless.[15]

Overall, China's military modernization efforts have given them a small increase in military capability, though not nearly enough to present a credible offensive threat to the region. In the next chapter, we examine how this slow increase in military capability affects the region and the implications of modernization for regional stability, regional security concerns, and U.S. policy.

Notes

[1] Paul H. B. Godwin and Dianne L. Smith, ed., *Asian Security to the Year 2000*, Department of Defense, December 15, 1996, n.p.; on-line, Internet, February 3, 1998, available from http://www.dodda.gov/asia_sec/2000-6/pau/

[2] Orville Schell, *Discos and Democracy, China in the Throes of Reform* (New York. Pantheon Books, 1988), 344-347.

[3] US Senate, *The Growth and Role of the Chinese Military: Hearing before the Subcommittee on East Asian and Pacific Affairs of the Committee on Foreign Relations,* 104th Cong., 1st sess., 1996, 50.

[4] Zalmay Khalilzad, ed., *Strategic Appraisal 1996* (Santa Monica, Ca.: Rand, 1996), 205-206.

[5] Richard A. Bitzinger and Bates Gill, *Gearing Up for High-Tech Warfare? Chinese and Taiwanese Defense Modernization and Implications for Military Confrontation Across the Taiwan Strait, 1995-2005* (Washington, D.C.: Center for Strategic and Budgetary Assessments, 1996), 21.

[6] Swanson Smith, "Chinese Defense Manufacturing in the Post Cold-War Era," *Military Capabilities of the World, 1996* (New York. Harper and Row, 1997), 78-80.

[7] US Senate, 116.

[8] US Congress, *Global Economic and Technological Change: Former Soviet Union, Central and Eastern Europe and China: Hearings before the Joint Economic Committee,* 103rd Cong., 2d sess., 1994.

[9] Ron Montaperto, "China as a Military Power," *Strategic Forum*, no. 56, December 1995, 1.

[10] Rick Fisher, Testimony to US Senate, *The Growth and Role of the Chinese Military: Hearing before the Subcommittee on East Asian and Pacific Affairs of the Committee on Foreign Relations,* 104th Cong., 1st sess., 1996, 30-36.

[11] James Nesmith, "China's Leader to Visit U.S.," *New York Times,* February 13, `1997.

[12] Khalilzad, 217.

[13] Khalilzad, 215.

[14] Bitzinger, 5.

[15] Ibid.

Chapter 7

Implications for the United States and the Region

China sees America snuggling up to India and kicking Pakistan in the shins, recognizing Vietnam, selling F-16s to Taiwan, walking hand-in-hand with Japan into the 21ˢᵗ century, wanting a united Korea under Seoul allied with the US. What does it look like from the Chinese perspective? A ring around China.[1]

—James Lilley, Former U.S. Ambassador to China

China's economic fundamentals are strong but its political system is weak.[2] Its territorial claims, lack of commitment to international security treaties, and force projection ambitions concern the U.S. as well as neighboring countries in the region. While Chinese defense modernization efforts have not yet produced a significant offensive force projection capability, it still may make significant progress in the medium to long term.[3] This would change the balance of power among nations of the region. Will China use this future capability to bully weaker states or use force to absorb Taiwan into the mainland?[4] This question, along with many others, is difficult to answer given the nature of Chinese international relations. According to Frankenstein and Gill,

> Is the true nature of the PLA the modernizing, aggressive force seen in its "pockets of excellence" and recently imported weapons – the atomic weapons, missiles, fighters, submarines, and rapid reaction units – or is it the bureaucratic, technology-inhibited organization that devotes at least as much time growing vegetables to make ends meet as it does to training? We find this duality in other aspects of [China]: consider the contrast between the China that is the world's fastest growing economy, and the China that is on the verge of peasant rebellion and worker unrest. Is China

39

the emergent hegemon, the threat none of its neighbors will talk about, or the benign engine driving future regional economic growth?[5]

The U.S. and the nations in the region should formulate foreign policy regarding China keeping two factors in mind. First, the U.S. cannot determine and should not waste time arguing about China's *intentions;* rather it must react to and deal only with China's *capabilities.* Secondly, the U.S. and regional countries should accept the fact that the national interests of the regional nations, the U.S., and China differ significantly. Sometimes these interests will conflict. As such, the regional actors should not regard China as an *enemy,* but merely another regional actor, albeit one with a different agenda.

In examining the first factor, China's future capabilities, Ron Montaperto asserts that with continued modernization efforts, they could develop adequate force projection capability in the coming decades.[6] In addition, China will be able to

1. Conduct low-level exercises and stage at-sea confrontations.[7]
2. Set up a naval blockade of Taiwan and other regional islands.[8]
3. Perform limited, regional missile attacks.[9]
4. Conduct limited offensive air strikes.[10]

The U.S. and regional players must develop a force structure to effectively deal with these increased military capabilities. In addition, they can take measures to ensure the continued peaceful coexistence of countries in the region through diplomatic and economic means.

Examining the second factor, the best way to ensure continued growth and peaceful coexistence in the region is to *engage* China in all diplomatic, economic, and regional security concerns. The U.S. should not regard the Chinese as its enemy, but as an extremely large trading partner. The policies should involve continued encouragement of China's cultural and economic interdependence with the rest of the region. It would include developing political relationships between China and neighboring countries. The regional powers should show a willingness to consider China's objectives as long as Beijing also respects the interests of the other parties. In addition, the U.S. and regional countries should explore the possibility of including China in a multilateral, regional security arrangement. However, all nations should resist all advanced technology arms sales to China. This will make Chinese military modernization more difficult and will allow additional time for the U.S. and regional actors to establish multilateral diplomatic, economic, and security arrangements.

In contrast to engagement, the U.S. should not embark on a containment policy. This would involve substantial investment in additional military forces for the U.S., which is not consistent with the current American military downsizing.[11] Also, it involves substantial increases in military presence in the area, something that the regional nations are likely to resist. This policy is also counterproductive. The mere perception of containment could force China to abandon economic reforms in favor of a faster military buildup, slowing the economic progress of the entire region. It could also solidify power for the ruling elite in China, thereby enabling them to hasten military modernization. It would also ensure the cooling of relations with the West. According to General Li Jijun, Vice President of the PLA's Academy of Military Science and one of China's most influential strategists, in a speech at the U.S. Army War College,

> Some rather perceptive people have pointed out that a policy of "containing" China is reminiscent of Cold War thinking. If ideology continues to divide our two countries, the consequences will be really undesirable. If you treat China as an enemy, you will have 1.2 billion enemies with which to contend...It is time to abandon Cold War thinking once and for all.[12]

So the U.S. and regional nations must walk a tightrope by forming a policy that maintains a balance of power so that China does not feel threatened, but at the same time, it does not see a power vacuum and an opportunity to stake additional claims in the region. The key to this engagement policy is time. It will take several years for China to develop the force projection capability it seeks. In the meantime, the nations of the region can engage China with mutual cooperation and coexistence, establishing ties and stabilizing relations. This concept is summarized best in a 1995 U.S. Government Accounting Office (GAO) report:

> At the PLA's current pace of modernization, the replacement of its 1950s and 1960s vintage equipment with more modern equipment will take years. Our current view is that China will not significantly increase its power projection capability in the near term. Thus, we have a window of opportunity to build the kind of relationship with China and its military that can lay the foundation for more confidence, cooperation, and stability in the future.[13]

This policy of engagement, backed up with matching military capability, is the best chance for the U.S. and regional nations to develop stronger relations with China and to allow the region to continue economic growth. In addition, it will foster the peace and stability necessary for the East Asian region to become a world economic center. The Cold War ended very peacefully; we can ill afford investment in a policy that could lead to a smaller, but maybe just as expensive, regional arms race.

Notes

[1] "Quotable Quotes," *The New York Times on the Web,* November 3, 1997, n.p.; on-line, Internet, January 8, 1998, available from http:///www.nytimes.com/cgi-bin/archives/tp_69a/gofoth/quotes/summ.

[2] Orville Schell, *Discos and Democracy, China in the Throes of Reform* (New York: Pantheon Books, 1988), 534.

[3] Zalmay Khalilzad, ed., *Strategic Appraisal 1996* (Santa Monica, Ca.: Rand, 1996), 214.

[4] John Bedford, People's Republic of China: U.S. Trade Partner or Threat to Our National Interests? (Carlisle Barracks, Pa.: U.S. Army War College, 1996), 2.

[5] John Frankenstein and Bates Gill, "Current and Future Challenges Facing Chinese Defense Industries," *China Quarterly*, June 1996, 426.

Notes

[6] Ron Montaperto, "China as a Military Power," *Strategic Forum*, no. 56, December 1995, 1.

[7] Samuel S. Kim, *China's Quest for Security in the Post-Cold War World* (Carlisle Barracks, Pa: U.S. Army War College, Strategic Studies Institute, 1996), 2.

[8] Richard A. Bitzinger and Bates Gill, *Gearing Up for High-Tech Warfare? Chinese and Taiwanese Defense Modernization and Implications for Military Confrontation Across the Taiwan Strait, 1995-2005* (Washington, D.C.: Center for Strategic and Budgetary Assessments, 1996), i.

[9] US House, *Security Challenges Posed by China: Hearing before the Committee on National Security*, 104th Cong., 2d sess., 1996, 20-22.

[10] Khalilzad, 211.

[11] R.W. Apple, Jr., "Analysis: Plenty of Process, but Little Progress." *The New York Times on the Web*, 30 October 1997, n.p.; on-line, Internet, 5 November 1997, available from http///www.nytimes.com/cpyint/30-10-97/anal3.

[12] Lt Gen Li Jijun, *Traditional Military Thinking and The Defensive Strategy of China. An Address at the U.S. Army War College*, ed. Earl H. Tilford, Jr. (Carlisle Barracks, Pa.: U.S. Army War College, Strategic Studies Institute, 1997), 9.

[13] US Senate, *The Growth and Role of the Chinese Military: Hearing before the Subcommittee on East Asian and Pacific Affairs of the Committee on Foreign Relations*, 104th Cong., 1st sess., 1996, 13.

Bibliography

Aporcho, Alfredo. "Worker Unrest Grows." *China Watch,* June 1996.

Bedford, John. *People's Republic of China: U.S. Trade Partner or Threat to Our National Interests?* Carlisle Barracks, Pa.: U.S. Army War College, 1996.

Binnendijk, Hans A. and Patrick L. Clawson, ed. *Strategic Assessment 1997: Flashpoints and Force Structure.* Washington, D.C.: National Defense University, Institute for National Strategic Studies, 1997.

Bitzinger, Richard A., and Bates Gill. *Gearing Up for High-Tech Warfare? Chinese and Taiwanese Defense Modernization and Implications for Military Confrontation Across the Taiwan Strait, 1995-2005.* Washington, D.C.: Center for Strategic and Budgetary Assessments, 1996.

Chagchu, Ti. "Defense Industries Help Country." *China Daily,* September 16, 1997.

Chan, Xia. "Jiang Zemin Addresses Party." *China Daily,* June 17, 1997.

Chu, Shulong. "The PRC Grids for Limited, High-Tech War." *Orbis*, Spring 1994..

Eikenberry, Karl W. *Explaining and Influencing Chinese Arms Transfers.* McNair Paper 36. Washington, D.C.: National Defense University, Institute for National Strategic Studies, 1996.

Fisher, Rick. Testimony to US Senate. *The Growth and Role of the Chinese Military: Hearing before the Subcommittee on East Asian and Pacific Affairs of the Committee on Foreign Relations.* 104th Cong., 1st sess., 1996.

Frankenstein, John and Bates Gill. "Current and Future Challenges Facing Chinese Defense Industries." *China Quarterly*, June 1996, 394-427.

Fung, Victor. "The Implications of China's Emergence." In *Overcoming Indifference.* New York: New York University Press, 1995.

Gill, Bates. "The Impact of Economic Reform Upon Chinese Defense Production." In *Military Modernization..* Edited by C. Dennison Lane, et al. London: T.J. Press, 1996.

Gill, Bates and Kim, Taeko. *China's Arms Acquisitions from Abroad: A Quest for "Superb and Secret Weapons."* SIPRI Research Report No. 11. New York: Oxford University Press, 1995.

Godwin, Paul H. B. and Dianne L. Smith, ed. *Asian Security to the Year 2000*, Department of Defense, December 15, 1996, n.p. On-line, Internet, February 3, 1998. Available from http://www.dodda.gov/asia_sec/2000-6/pau/

Gurtov, Mel. "Swords into Market Shares: China's Conversion of Military Industry to Civilian Production." *China Quarterly*, June 1993, 213-241.

Holmes, Kim R., and James J. Przystup, ed. *Between Diplomacy and Deterrence. Strategies for U.S. Relations with China.* ISBN 0-89195-242-X. May 1997. On-line, Internet, February 3, 1998. Available from http://www.heritage/pubs_library/chinabook/

"Jiang: U.S. Has Nothing to Fear." *Associated Press On-Line*, November 1, 1997, n.p. On-line. Prodigy News Service, 6 November 1997.

Jijun, Lt Gen Li. *Traditional Military Thinking and The Defensive Strategy of China.* An Address at the U.S. Army War College. Edited by Earl H. Tilford, Jr. Carlisle Barracks, Pa.: U.S. Army War College, Strategic Studies Institute, 1997.

Khalilzad, Zalmay, ed. *Strategic Appraisal 1996.* Santa Monica, Ca.: Rand, 1996.

Kim, Samuel S. *China's Quest for Security in the Post-Cold War World.* Carlisle Barracks, Pa: U.S. Army War College, Strategic Studies Institute, 1996.

Kondapalli, Srikanth. "China's Defense Industry." *Strategic Analysis*, September 1996, 863-884.

Lane, C. Dennison, Mark Weisenbloom, and Dimon Liu, ed. *Chinese Military Modernization.* London: TJ Press, 1996.

Lichu, Chihai. "New Directions from Beijing." *China Daily,* June 17,1997.

Lilley, James. "Foreword," In *Military Modernization.* Edited by C. Dennison Lane, et al. London: T.J. Press, 1996.

Montaperto, Ron. "China as a Military Power." *Strategic Forum*, no. 56 (Dec 1995): 1-4.

Nesmith, James. "China's Leader to Visit U.S." *New York Times,* February 13,1997.

"Quotable Quotes." *New York Times on the Web,* November 3, 1997, n.p. On-line. Internet, January 8, 1998. Available from http///www.nytimes.com/cgi-bin/archives/tp_69a/gofoth/quotes/summ.

Pondelton, Charles, ed. *World Statistics, 1997.* New York, N.Y.: Random House, 1997.

Rejeako, Sperric. "China Changes Course." *China Watch,* March 1993.

Sanger, David E. "Market Reform Irreversible, Chinese Leader Tells U.S." *The New York Times on the Web*, September 27, 1997, n.p. On-line. Internet, 6 November 1997. Available from http//www.nytimes.com/news/27-09-97/hdl.

Schell, Orville. *Discos and Democracy. China in the Throes of Reform.* New York. Pantheon Books, 1988.

Shambaugh, David, ed. *Greater China: The Next Superpower?* New York: Oxford University Press, 1995.

Shambaugh, David and Zhongchun, Wang. *China's Transition into the 21st Century: U.S. and PRC Perspectives.* Carlisle Barracks, Pa.: U.S. Army War College, Strategic Studies Institute, 1996.

Shultz, John. Testimony to US Senate. *The Growth and Role of the Chinese Military: Hearing before the Subcommittee on East Asian and Pacific Affairs of the Committee on Foreign Relations.* 104th Cong., 1st sess., 1996.

Smith, Albert. "Chinese Industries Enter the Free-Market." *New York Times on the Web,* November 3, 1997, n.p. On-line. Internet, November 16, 1997. Available from http///www.nytimes.com/03-11-97.

Smith, Swanson. "Chinese Defense Manufacturing in the Post Cold-War Era." *Military Capabilities of the World, 1996.* New York. Harper and Row, 1997.

Sutter, Robert and Mitchener, Peter. *China's Rising Military Power and Influence: Issues and Options for the U.S.* Washington, D.C.: Congressional Research Service, 1996.

US Congress. Global Economic and Technological Change: Former Soviet Union, Central and Eastern Europe and China: Hearings before the Joint Economic Committee. 103rd Cong., 2d sess., 1994.

US Defense Intelligence Agency. *Defense Industries in Transition.* (PC-1920-59D-95). Washington, D.C.: Government Printing Office, 1995.

US House. Security Challenges Posed by China: Hearing before the Committee on National Security. 104th Cong., 2d sess., 1996.

US Senate. The Export of Supercomputers to China: Implications for Peace and Security: Prepared for delivery to the Subcommittee on International Security, Proliferation, and Federal Service, by Stephen D. Bryen. 105th Cong., 1st sess., 1997.

US Senate. The Growth and Role of the Chinese Military: Hearing before the Subcommittee on East Asian and Pacific Affairs of the Committee on Foreign Relations. 104th Cong., 1st sess., 1996.

Weileng, Xiano. "Premier Draws Praise." *China Daily,* January 4, 1993.

Wu, Ling. "Economic Policies." *China Daily,* September 13, 1997.